EMAIL MARKETING TECHNIQUES

Email Marketing Beginner's Guide and Strategies

By Paul D. Kings

Copyrights 2017 **Paul D. Kings**

https://www.pauldkings.com

Subscribe to my newsletter to
get free information and free books on
MAKING MONEY online.

Table of Contents

PREFACE

Want to know the smart email marketing technique that will double your revenue instantly? Then, this book is a must read for your needs. You've heard it before... "The money is in the list." It's a common phrase that is thrown around the internet marketing circles each and everyday. For newbies trying to earn money online, those who are truly trying to understand what this means, they find themselves unable to earn the kind of money that many people only dream of.

If you are entering the world of online marketing, then chances are that you already know that you can't get very far without planning and using effective email marketing techniques. Unfortunately, this is such a broad topic that many people don't even know where to begin. This book will help you if you are a beginner and also if you have learned by the school of hard knocks to figure some of it out on your own.

It is common to find techniques that might apply to some industries or fields, but which do not apply to others. Look, there is no doubt that this is a confusing and often complex topic. By following some common sense techniques and practices highlighted in this book, you really can make your email marketing campaign more seamless, less work, and quite profitable.

CHAPTER 1- WHAT IS EMAIL MARKETING?

You may have asked yourself the question about what email marketing entails. You may also have even heard this term many times before, but were unable to grasp the real concept and importance behind it. As the name suggests, this type of marketing uses email to communicate a company's brand, products, and snapshots of its advertising campaign. This way of communication enables you to send promotional messages directly to your clients or target market and to give them a call to action to respond to your campaign.

You can also send email messages to people you want to acquire as potential future customers or your targeted customers. By frequently sending this promotional emails, you can remind current clients to return and make purchases again, because most customers forget where they got an item and will go get it from a familiar source if they are reminded. This enables you to strengthen your relationships with all of your past and present customers. It also helps to builds brand and product loyalty which is important in retaining customers.

Before this type of online communication became an everyday part of life, companies would send promotional materials through the regular postal system, this promotional material was delivered in millions of mail boxes across the country. We now call this method snail mail and it used up lot of manpower, paper, and time. Sending advertising content by email is more practical and cost effective than mailing promotional materials by snail mail---and it can be automated so that you set it up and it happens automatically.

Another way businesses used to disperse marketing materials is through printed newsletters. Some companies also used to insert advertising leaflets and coupons between magazine pages and newspapers. Imagine the labor needed to accomplish that arduous task, what a hassle and most of it was just circular filed on the customer end, so it was not very effective. Now, it is also more environmentally friendly to send emails because it is paperless, saving trees, time, manpower, money, and has a higher response rate than snail mail.

Brand recognition and product recognition require repeated exposures to be effective, sending promotional letters by email is much cheaper than other forms of communication or advertising. With email, you also get to reach out to specific customers directly, your targeted customers. Posting large billboards or ads on websites will require your target market to visit the site of the billboard or the website to see what you are offering, thus limiting how many of your actual target customers will be exposed to your brand or product.

Due to the nature of our technological world, emails land directly on your customers' laptop or computer monitor so that your target customers are politely forced to interact with your email. Customers tend to check their inbox at least once a day, and there is very little chance that your message will be missed. Within email advertising, there are different types of email marketing campaigns. The main types are called direct marketing, retention email marketing, and indirect marketing or advertising through other people's emails.

Direct marketing involves sending promotional material to clients that announce your company's special discount, freebie, buy one get one offer, or other special offer. These are usually sent to a list of customers whom you already have names and emails of, these are usually your repeat customers who do not need to be convinced of your brand or product, because they are already your customers. You can also buy a list of emails to send out to potential new customers, who may not know your brand or product already.

Retention marketing, on the other hand, takes the form of e-newsletters which are sent regularly to your current customers to get them to stay your customers, just to remember you and not to get seduced by a different company or brand. Retention email does not just contain an encouragement to buy something, with a particular call to action, but usually contains informative material that will be of use to your customer to keep you at the top of their mind when they have a need.

Indirect marketing involves advertising through other customers's email, actually your target customer's email. It is a prudent way of promoting your brand, company, product, or service. Your ads will be discreetly inserted into your target customer's emails that are sent to their friends and family. By using this type of email marketing, you are using your customer's trust level with their friends to transfer some of that trust to your brand or product.

Basically, this is the answer to your question about what email marketing involves. This kind of advertising is usually done with the recipient's permission to receive the messages. There should always be an option in the email for the recipient to opt out of receiving your promotional messages. That way they feel that they have control of the communication with you and that they are receiving your email as long as it provides something that benefits them.

Many times Safe Unsubscribe and other options will be available as to keep the relationship with your customer's friend as polite and permissive as possible. This helps to keep your messages out of their SPAM folder and from alerting the email carriers (Gmail, Yahoo, etc) that you are sending SPAM. The point is to keep enough of these emails going to the target customer's friends and family without being flagged in the process.

Advantages of Email Marketing

The DMA (Direct Marketing Association) tells us that ninety-percent of companies use email marketing. They describe email marketing as the new hero for troubled financial times, because it cuts the budget on supplies, manpower, and time spent on marketing to get each customer. Their research shows that more than half of companies surveyed expect to increase their spending on direct email this year. Because of the targeting aspect of email and the increased exposure return, many companies are cutting back on traditional direct mail (snail mail) in order to do more email campaigns. That's the trend and the statistics, but why is email marketing the answer for your business?

There are several massive advantages to email marketing compared to traditional marketing techniques:

First of all, its inexpensive because the cost of email marketing campaigns is significantly less per customer generated than other marketing strategies. As the medium is so scalable, you also have the ability to commit as much or as little as you want to email marketing.

Secondly, it is a great Return On Investment. No other type of direct marketing will offer the same sort of ROI as email marketing. This is partly because the average cost per customer is so low. You aren't spending as much in the first place for the campaign and you are targeting a pre-qualified set of potential customers.

Third, the flexibility of the email campaigns also has a huge impact, because targeted email marketing allows you to personalise campaigns to your customers. When you know part of their needs would be met by your brand, product or services, and you can personalize the email to meet that specific need, you will reap more customers per marketing dollar.

Fourth, it is also a great way to maintain the relationships with your existing customers and to make them aware of new offers, products, or services. When done right, email marketing can give you a great return on investment. What's the catch? You have to do it right because if you get it wrong, you can turn off your current customers. If you don't have any in-house experience with email marketing campaigns, then it can be wise to take expert advice on how to incrementally phase in your new products and services with your current customers so that they do not become confused about your brand or abandon the previous products you used to sell them.

Fifth, an email campaign allows you to measure its effectiveness more than any other type of direct marketing. And this measurable quality is unbiased. A marketing executive can lie with statistics, saying their campaign is performing well, but with an email campaign you are able to track every opened email, every click, every email shared right through to the sale. This differs massively from a direct mail snail mail campaign where no one can tell you how many went straight into the trash bin. With email campaigns, you can see if your campaign has worked, but perhaps more importantly you can see where it didn't work and what didn't work about it. This allows you to learn from experience and use that feedback to tailor your email activity to your customers needs and their responses to your products and services.

Nobody will tell you they like spam email. What do we actually mean by spam? Spam used to mean that an email was sent to your email without you requesting it. But in the world of sponsored ads and Facebook placed ads, requesting something is not even a dominant part of our current technology world. We don't expect to request everything we get.

At the moment, opinion is shifting towards the idea of spam being an email that is irrelevant or not useful to the user. We have lowered our standards from 'I didn't ask for that' permission based expectations to 'I don't have any use for that' utility based expectations. Don't let this change in consumer expectations lull you into a false sense of security. A recent DMA survey showed that seventy-five percent of consumers found less than twenty-percent of emails they received to be relevant to them.

This change seems to focus around the difference between the Millenial Generation with the GenX Generation and their opposite, the Baby Boomers. For Millenials and GenX consumers, they don't expect as much privacy, permission, or context to their interactions. They thrive in the environments of texting and email because they can do things quickly without the hassle of politeness and context.

The Baby Boomer Generation craves context, politeness, permission, and security. They are the ones who still class spam as something they didn't sign up for. Baby Boomers were used to a much more polite and permissive, high-context environment that predated all of the social media and email campaigns. This is also why they don't respond as well to texting. The context of a communication, its intent, is important to these consumers.

If a Baby Boomer perceives an email as being unsolitited, even if it is for something they want or a brand they trust, they will reject it, because it is not considered polite. They feel invaded by that contact. It is the equivalent in dating of "I want to be kissed, but I don't want to be kissed by YOU."

Another study asked consumers to rate acceptability of promotional emails out of five (five is most acceptable, one is least acceptable.) Permission clearly made marketing emails more acceptable, where the consumer had given permission for ongoing communication participants rated it as four-point-one out of five.

On the other hand, when the consumer had interacted with a company, but had not given permission for contact, the score dropped significantly to two-point-five. The worst score was for marketing campaigns generated by companies which had not been given permission and with whom the consumer had never interacted. This scored one-point-seven out of five and it makes sense, there was no context and no trust established.

The moral of this email marketing story seems clear. Spend your time, money, and manpower to concentrate on targeted email marketing campaigns. This will make your email more relevant to your potential customers and will focus on opt-in permission (and trust) generated lists. This seems like the proper way to make sure your emails are not classed as spam by any potential customer's definition.

Disadvantages of Email Marketing

One of the main disadvantages of email marketing is spam, which in this expectation is unsolicited email sent in bulk. Technology and customers really struggle with this. On one hand, it really hampers genuine efforts to communicate with your target customer, since the sheer bulk of spam emails can be so frustrating that customers can often mistake genuine commercial email, such as a mailing list that they may be subscribed to, for spam.

In a world where Nigerian Prince's are trying to get someone, anyone, to receive their millions of dollars urgently and other such scams, customers and their email technology has had to become more cautious. The spam/scam cycle has led to customers and email hosting companies utilizing spam filters. This has a negative effect on genuine email marketers, because their emails often get filtered out by these spam filters. Apart from spam, another drawback to email marketing is that the sheer volume of commercial email that people get in a day, so much so, it can often result in them deleting them without even a glance.

Email marketing has transformed the way business is done. Sure, there are some disadvantages, but even so, it must be said that the impact of this instantaneous marketing has had on business is largely positive. It has had a clear edge over many types of marketing communication. Hence, email marketing is here to stay for a long time indeed.

Bulk Email Marketing

What is bulk email marketing? How does it differ from regular email marketing? Bulk email marketing is a method of reaching and communicating with potential customers. Unlike targeted email marketing, this type of email is less likely to be targeted to a specific group or consumer type or to have permission from the receiver. It is the scattershot of all email marketing, similar to cold calling in phone marketing. It culls any email address that can be found or bought and sends out a genereric brand or product advertisement. If someone responds or buys the product, they are moved to a targeted email list and nurtured from sale to sale. Bulk email marketing is primarily used to gauge interest in a brand, product, or service.

Over the last decade, bulk email marketing has become a big business. Various studies have reported that an average bulk email campaign yields a one to two percent response, which does not seem like a high response rate until you multiply that back against the gigantic numbers of emails sent out with little effort or expense. This return on investment makes the bulk email marketing one of the least expensive methods of email marketing, even less than traditional bulk postage mail.

There are a few disadvantages to bulk email marketing. For instance, unsolicited emails are often labeled 'spam' emails, and it may affect the company's reputation as customers generally disapprove of this type of email being received without permission. Not only that, but many states and locales have decided to limit or outright ban the sending of unsolicited spam email campaigns by customers for profit or otherwise, so you should check your local and state laws for guidelines.

Although bulk email marketing is very effective, some points should be considered before implementing it. The content of the email should be very crisp and to the point. Avoid the usage of attachments or complex graphics because it takes more space, requires some time to download, and spam filters sometimes automatically flag emails going to many customers at once who have these features.

Potential customers generally will not read anything unsolicited, if it takes even a moment of effort. So, your email has to be fun, funny, witty, charming, provocative, interesting, and engaging in the first few seconds, otherwise it is deleted. You have to make sure that any hyperlinks to your products, services or website provided in the emails are functioning properly. You should address the recipient by first name. And, the subject line of your email should be short, catchy, and to the point.

Complaints about unsolicited emails from many customers may result in blocking your account by your internet service provider (ISP). If your account gets blocked by your internet service provider, you will have to bypass the point of origin of your email and go through a virtual private network (VPN) and all traffic coming from your computer will be redirected over that network and bounced around so that your internet service provider won't be able to tell where you are coming from. But that is more complex than this book would allow to go into. Suffice to say, prevent getting blocked by your internet service provider because it is a headache to create the work arounds and protocols to get your marketing done.

How to Start a Bulk Email Marketing Campaign Without Becoming a Spammer

Bulk email marketing is the technique of marketing your brand, products or services through email by sending emails to hundreds, if not thousands, of email addresses at the same time. The time to set up is minimal and the returns can be great. The method of doing this simply requires an email server to send bulk emails from and a robust list of email addresses to market them to.

It is an ingenious and simple technique that doesn't cost the spammer any money (except you may buy the email addresses initially) and is so advanced that, if it is done right, it can be said that it has even been able to go around the law. This does not mean that some spammers have not been caught for the practice, but indicates that a large amount of spam and spammers are virtually untraceable.

Many bulk email marketers have teamed up with malware authors and spyware and virus engineers to bypass the protections and get into servers and send mass emails to all who use the server for emailing.

This is the reason that open relay servers are hardly used any more, because hijacking the system in this way to 'launder' or disguise spam emails has become such a problem that the internet service providers are putting increased protections on their servers to make it harder to use these bypass techniques.

Considering all the problems and perceptions involved with spam emailing, and bulk email marketing in general, the question is whether it is a good medium to indulge in as an online marketer. This is a complex question. The question itself begs the next question of whether people will buy your brand, product, or service that they get information about from an unknown email. The answer is that it depends.

Bulk email campaigns can work, they just have to be done in the right way and with the RIGHT brand, product or service. They are seen to be most effective at promoting completely unknown brands who need that initial exposure in the market to a broad audience for basic brand recognition. They would not be good for promoting already widely known brands because it doesn't solve the marketing problem for a known brand. But an unknown brand, it can kick the 'what's that' factor up and create an initial buzz about the brand that was not there before.

Bulk email campaigns are best to market specific products, especially products with a highly motivated customer, such as for weight loss, diet supplements, male enhancement or function medicines, hair loss supplements or cosmetics, etc. These are consumers who are much less likely to care if they know or trust the source of the email because they have tried many products which may, or may not have worked, and they are eager to try something else that will work. These consumers consider trying different products until they find the right one an 'opportunity cost' and it makes them more likely to click and buy from an unknown source.

With bulk email campaigns for service promotion, this works well because the consumer has an individual or company, the service provider, whom they will be able to get satisfaction from if the service does not go as planned. The consumer is bargaining that they can click on the bulk email, get a service at a price they would like to pay, and then force the service provider to satisfy their promise that was marketed in the bulk email. In the era of a global review community, they are right because a service provider can spoil their company's reputation with providing too many shoddy services and getting hit with a tsunami of bad reviews.

So, you need to do it right by creating and maintaining a bulk email marketing campaign with quality targeted email addresses, which are opted-in email addresses. The US government has legislated that it is not illegal to send email as part of the bulk mailing campaign, however, that there should be an unsubscribe option available in the mail for the users' benefit. Additionally, you should ensure that the email addresses that you do acquire are done legitimately and not from hacking into servers.

One of the best tools to ensure that you get qualified and targeted email addresses for sending bulk emails is to start a page on a popular networking site. This is a good forum to advertise and build a following for your brand, product, or service. The only way that you will then contact these potential customers is by using the platform's mailing software of the networking site. At the end of the day, it is like legal spam.

Another option as a serious online marketer is to forge meaningful, symbiotic tie-ups with other companies that already have a set customer base that you can tap into. If you position yourself correctly, you can even ride along on the other brand's goodwill to ensure that your potential customers are properly targeted and that you have a receptive audience.

In this age of online marketing, bulk email marketing to unsolicited emails is a technique that is fast fading in popularity and acceptance. Most spam emailers that send bulk emails are getting blocked by sophisticated software and wise customers, which is reducing the effectiveness globally.

CHAPTER 2- EMAIL MARKETING TECHNIQUES

Email marketing is usually free from monetary investment. Almost all business owners use this strategy to stay in touch with their existing customers and to attract new business as well. Email marketing techniques are something that seems to be quite easy, which leads alot of people think that it's just about sending out their promo emails to their customers. Simple and done, right?

To be done effectively, this is not actually true. To generate a good return on your time and energy investment, it is very necessary that you utilize more sophisticated email marketing techniques. Such techniques help you in enhancing the overall probability of potential customers to open and read your mails. I will present some of the best practices and email marketing techniques that are widely recommended by marketing experts.

Best Practices and Strategies for Email Marketing Success

Email marketing is one of the most profitable strategies available to the online entrepreneur (and brick and mortar business owners, too). Consider this: About ninety-nine percent of your website visitors will leave without buying anything from you on their first visit. But by creating an attractive and compelling opt-in offer, you can at least get their contact details. Then you can use email marketing to follow up on their interest, build relationships, and turn them into paying customers.

And email marketing is by far the BEST and CHEAPEST way to stay in touch with your customers and build rock-solid relationships with them -- so they'll buy from you again and again! This is called the "lifetime value" of your customers, and it's extremely profitable.

Email marketing just plain works! Just take a look at these statistics from PostFuture:

There are now more than 1 BILLION Internet users worldwide -- and ninety percent of them use email.

- Seventy percent of users receive opt-in email from online businesses.

- Eighty-two percent of online buyers have made at least one purchase in response to an email promotion.
- Thirty-two percent have made an immediate online purchase in response to an email.

With numbers like these, you can understand why I'm always stunned to hear about a business that STILL hasn't started to take advantage of email marketing strategies.

If you're stuck for ideas on how to use email marketing to ramp up your profits, here are ten proven email marketing strategies to get you started...

Email marketing strategy #1: Develop relationships and establish credibility by offering free valuable information to your customers.

Sending your subscribers valuable, free information -- such as a authoritative eBook – which will help them get to know and trust you. Once you've established your credibility, you dramatically increase your chances of converting subscribers into lifelong customers. You can offer anything of value that can be produced by you. It can be a free report or a free trial version of your app or software... whatever you think your subscribers would like that will create good will between you and them!

Email marketing strategy #2: Encourage repeat customers by announcing regular specials.

Once you've started collecting email addresses, you can send your customers and subscribers regular updates letting them know what your online-only specials are. If these deals can be gotten a different way, then there is no reason for your customer to keep paying attention to your email. If you keep sending exclusive discount offers through email, then they continue to see value in the communication. It is a great way to get your customers familiar with your brand, products, services, your website -- and turn them into repeat customers who will buy from you again and again.

Email marketing strategy #3: Host Exclusive "Customer Only" events.

Everyone wants to feel special and like they are in an exclusive club or group. Suppose you own a restaurant and you've been collecting your customers' email addresses, you could send each of them an email invitation to an exclusive wine-tasting evening for regular diners only. Rewards like this are one of the best ways to capitalize on the lifetime value of your customers and to reinforce to your customer the value of opening your emails.

If you own an online business, you can set up a special page on your site that is accessible only to customers, a login only page -- and then send them a email telling them how to take advantage of the specials you advertise and post only on that page.

Email marketing strategy #4: Include promotions in your appointment reminders.

If you are running a service based business, as opposed to a product driven retail business, you can still capitalize on the power of email marketing by sending appointment reminders to your clients.

If you're a karate teacher, for example, you could send your new clients an email three days before their first lesson, reminding them where you are located and when they need to do when they arrive. In that same message, you could include a coupon that offers them twenty-five percent off their lessons if they bring a friend to enroll as well! This works better for you, because if they bring a friend then they are more likely to show up to their first lesson, stick with your service for a longer period of time, and to go to you over your competitor because of the discount. The lifetime value of that customer just increased.

Email marketing strategy #5: Follow up immediately with your hottest customer or sale leads

You can use email to follow up with people you have spoken with personally, but who have not yet made a purchase from your business. You can offer to answer any additional questions that they may have, and let them know that you are available to speak with them at their convenience. This can dramatically increase your chances of closing a sale by providing your leads with extra information and attention that they're not expecting.

Email marketing strategy #6: Offer electronic "loyalty coupons".

This is a great way to get your existing customers to buy from you again and again. Simply send each of your customers a coupon that they can show on their phone screen at the point of sale in your business, or print and bring with them into your brick and mortar store, or input into your company website. It is always a good idea to make your coupons valid for a limited time in order to motivate your customers to make a purchase from you as soon as possible.

Email marketing strategy #7: Send follow-up offers to your customers

Follow-up offers are one of the most powerful ways to build a profitable business. It is rare to have a product or service that a customer only needs once, so whatever the obsolescence of the product or service you offer is, make your follow up on that interval. This builds on the trust you've established to close the initial sale -- and turn first-time buyers into regular customers. For example, if you provide oil changes, the customary return time for another oil change would be three months. Just before the customer's three month time-lapse, send them an email for five-dollars off an oil change and make the expiration in two weeks. This motivates them to return to you, on schedule, and not to go to one of your competitors.

How profitable can follow-up email be? My team once sent our targeted new customers a follow-up email introducing them to a product that we thought they might like. The entire process of writing the email and sending it out to these customers took about twenty minutes -- and the result was a direct profit of $74,000!

Email marketing strategy #8: Encourage "Refer a Friend" Discounts or Promotions

Email is a great way to encourage referrals because it's easy for people to forward messages to their families, friends, and coworkers. Make sure every newsletter, offer, or eBook you send to your subscribers reminds them that they can forward your message to anyone they think might be interested. You could even run a promotion that gives your existing customers something for free every time they personally refer new customer to you. The only caveat with this is running afoul of anti-kickback laws.

Email marketing strategy #9: Deliver your product electronically.

Suppose you've written a book and you're currently selling paperback copies through your site for $29 each. By creating a digital version of your book -- which is WAY easier than you're probably thinking -- you can simply email it to your customers. And since you won't have to worry about things like printing costs, warehousing, packaging, and delivery, you can DRAMATICALLY increase your profit margin and get double return on your time investment by having the book available in two forms!

Email marketing strategy #10: Use email to sell your knowledge and create recurring revenue

If you are an expert on a particular topic -- and just about everyone is -- then you've got a successful business based on a paid-subscription newsletter waiting to be born. There are many sites to do this with, one that has a stable platform, where you can gather 'patrons' and get feedback from your target community is Patreon (https://www.patreon.com/). This site is very flexible and will allow you to do a paid subscription with it being hosted there and they handle most of the headaches, because it is already hooked to WordPress and paypal and all the amenities you would need.

Of course, there are tons of other email marketing strategies you can put to use. And once you realize just how easy it is to use email marketing to drive sales, you'll be thinking of all kinds of new strategies yourself!

Targeted Direct Email marketing system

As a marketing strategy that uses emails to reach out to the customers directly, the targeted direct email marketing is an effective form of marketing. The prime reason behind the strategy proving effective, is the huge returns that businesses gain on their investment of mostly time. Sending targeted emails is a way of segmenting the market and appealing to your relevant and motivated customers.

With the concept of mass un-targeted marketing losing its sheen, companies are looking for alternative marketing strategies that help identify and reach their target customers. Therefore, the strategy of using targeted direct emails has grown organically as a feasible option. Many sources online, such as Google and Facebook will sell you their search engine information to refine your marketing. Most of this information you can figure out on your own without paying them, but it takes a little technology savvy.

The development in technology has led to the refinement in the direct marketing approach. Today there are many kinds of software which help in capturing email leads and to refine your marketing words to benefit from search engine trends. It helps to compile a list of customers to be targeted. Many agencies carry out the task of targeted marketing with the help of emails for their client companies. These agencies generate emails that provide data which is relevant to the needs of customers. Instead of just advertising the services or products of a company, these agencies generate information rich content that might be useful for the customers. They don't just stuff the customers with information.

E-Newsletters

E-newsletters help build a strong and loyal customer base, keep them informed, and keep your brand and product at the top of their mind. This allows for an improved and efficient service which can be provided to a select group of customers. With a constant focus on a specific group of customers, the services offered to them can be enhanced considerably. Moreover, word-of-mouth publicity by loyal customers helps increase your business, because these super-fans become your unpaid marketing agents. According to experts working in the field of targeted direct email marketing, it is possible to earn between 50 cents and one-dollar per subscriber per month.

Copywriting

The component of 'article writing' can be successfully incorporated into your marketing strategy in order to increase the web traffic to your website and elevate the status of your website in the ranking of the search engines. If you don't personally have this skill set, seeking the help of a copywriter to develop your content is a smart move. Contracting an experienced writer helps generate relevant and quality content for email campaigns and frees you up to take care of the rest of your business.

It is also crafty to take advantage of a new trend in advertising: Advertorials. These are articles which on the surface look like news or at the very least editorials, but they are really targeted advertising. For certain, you may need the help of a professional writer to get this right. Advertorials will need enough fact based information and topic research layered with product recommendations which solve the article's underlying problem—and to engage your reader to solve their own problem with YOUR product. It requires a bit more work, but it pays dividends.

Branding

Sending targeted emails is a smart way to build your brand or product recognition. When a customer is targeted repetitively by your brand for him to recognize and remember the company's service, there are increased chances that he would go with the service that is fresh in the mind. In general, customers are lazy. It is the 'closest donut' principle. If a person drives by a donut store every day on the way to work and on the way home, they will most likely go to that donut shop when they have a craving. Not because they are the best donuts in town, but because they are the most familiar to the customer. Be their 'Closest Donut' in your advertising. Stay on their mind in the background, waiting for their need to arise so that they unconsciously choose you to do business with.

Keeping Your Customer Informed

Direct email marketing is an effective means of keeping your customers informed about company policies. It helps build trust about the company in the minds of customers, because they feel like they are on the inner part of your circle. The strategy of using targeted direct email marketing is effective in finding new customers, as well as retaining your repeating customers. Efficient use of the techniques listed above will definitely help in boosting your business.

How to Choose the Best Email Marketing Platform

You'll often hear in internet marketing circles that, "The money is in the list." For that reason, building up a list of email subscribers forms a part of most online businesses' internet marketing management strategy. Having worked with several email marketing platforms over the years, I thought I'd share my thoughts on various criteria for making a smart choice for an email service provider.

Deliverability

First of all, know that ISPs (Internet Service Providers) partly have the interests of their customers in mind and they also have their own reputation in mind. To them, spam is anything the subscriber doesn't want in his or her inbox. Therefore, deliverability of your emails will partly be based on your own reputation, as the ISPs perceive it. Have you built a relationship with your subscribers, creating practical expectations and then meeting them with relevant, value-added content?

However, it's also based on the reputation of your email marketing service provider. For many years, the realm of ISPs, Google through its Gmail platform has dominated Yahoo in spam detection and prevention, along with scam detection and prevention. Many users who want a SPAM-free email will look at the ISP and figure out which one has put the most research and development into making sure emails which the email user has requested get through to them and the spam gets blocked.

One thing to ask yourself when starting an email campaign through an ISP: Do they take a active role in meeting CAN-SPAM guidelines and building win-win relationships between ISPs and businesses? It's worth finding this out, because all the great content in the world has limited value if much of it goes undelivered and ends up in the spam folder.

If you are developed in your email marketing, more than a true beginner, and want to take your email marketing up a notch then AWeber is a leader in interfacing with more well-developed and more frequently visited websites. The cost is reasonable if you have more than 1,000 targeted visitors to your site per day. It will allow you to have your targeted-customers sign up for your newsletters or your campaigns and for you to manage them efficiently through their service in a semi-automated manner.

Capability and Flexibility

The various email marketing platforms all have their own strengths and limitations. Here are some scenarios, decide which one you fit into most closely and then you will see the solution that fits your needs:

I have a single email list. I want to create a short (five messages or less) autoresponder series for new subscribers.

Solution: A service such as Constant Contact may work well for you.

I want the ability to create multiple, unique lists within a single account. It is it important to me to be able to segment these lists and adjust my marketing messages to subscribers' behavior. I want a platform that can integrate with other service providers, such as 1shoppingcart.com.

Solution: AWeber may be the best service provider for you.

I sell multiple products and want a particularly robust system that ties together a shopping cart, email marketing platform, POP email accounts, calendar, task management, and more, in a single, cloud-based solution.

Solution: InfusionSoft may be the answer for you.

Naturally, the best solution for your business is going to depend on your individual needs and those MAY change as your business develops and you become more sophisticated in your marketing. The important thing is to think through what your needs are...and what you anticipate them to be in a couple of years, so that you can scale the solution to your now needs and your future needs. Because thinking short term is not a good option. It's a fairly major undertaking to migrate your subscriber list from one service provider to another, so you want to find a solution that's sufficiently robust for now and later, without swinging too far in the opposite direction and overbuying.

Ease of Use and Quality of Training

This is highly subjective, of course, but here are a couple of things to consider when you're choosing the service provider for the email marketing branch of your internet marketing management plan. How do you learn best? For example, do you like to learn by reading instructions or by watching videos? If you prefer live training (for instance, by webinar), is this type of training offered? What support does the provider offer to help you hit the ground running with their service? Is this included in the monthly subscription fee, or does training incur an additional fee? Another place to look is on the service provider's blog and help resources, if they have one. The quality of the content there can give you hints about what you can expect later.

Quality of Technical Support

Finally, you want to be assured that when you're stuck, effective help is going to be available. A great way to check on what other customers are saying about a service provider is to do a keyword search in one of the major social media channels.

It isn't necessarily a red flag, if a problem is noted there, but it can lead you to do more research. In fact, it's particularly enlightening to see how the provider handles it when a problem does arise. Other things to think about may include whether technical support is included in your subscription fee, what their support hours are, and where the support is based.

For instance, if you're on Pacific Time and your email marketing platform's live technical support is available 9am to 5pm Eastern Time, that's something you might want to be aware of. It's not necessarily a deal-breaker, but it's good to know ahead of time, before you need them and they are closed. As another example, if you're going to incur an additional cost for live technical support, does it involve a separate monthly fee, or can you pay by the incident or trouble ticket?

Making the Choice

If your internet marketing management strategy includes email marketing, you want the solution that provides the best combination of features, ease-of-use, cost, and support. With some good planning and research, you can uncover the best solution for your unique needs.

CHAPTER 3- WHAT IS AN AUTORESPONDER.

Auto-responders are messages set to go out automatically based on certain input parameters. They help you automate campaigns and manage one-to-one communication with your recipients.

They are sent to your contacts in a sequence at intervals calculated starting from the day a contact opts into your campaign e.g. Day zero, the day they contact your website (instant message), Day three, Day seven, Day fourteen, Day twenty-one. Auto-responders are useful if you want to send an automatic message of a certain type to contacts who join your list. When you set up an auto-responder cycle, messages will go out on a specific day of a contact's subscription period.

Best AutoResponder For Your Business

Have you recently started a online business? If yes, then I am sure you are looking for some help to increase your web traffic and to convert those potential customers to actual customers for your business. One of the options, which you may want to consider is the use of an autoresponder software. It is an automated response system that sends out email messages to a particular mailing list, which is an easy and effective solution for business communication.

This scheduled and controlled email message system is written and planned well in advance. With this service, you will not have to sit and send a big list of emails manually. You will be able to send out emails to many costumers or clients without a second thought, truly 'set it and forget it' style. Now that we have agreed that it is a great way of promoting your business, let me compare for you the best ones in the business.

AutoResponder Software Review

There are three basic types of autoresponder softwares on the market: free, scripts and remote autoresponder software. Each one of them has its own positive and negative aspects. Here are some of the most popular softwars with their high and low aspects in detail.

Aweber

If you are full-time internet marketer and need to correspond with your clients everyday with a robust system, then you may want to consider Aweber. Their services are approximately $30 per month for the full range of functions. Unlike many of the free auto responding softwares, Aweber ensures emails are delivered.

Its online interface and marketing tools are user-friendly, and forms can be set up as well. There is the direct sign-up form for the customer's website. Apart from emails, there are other services which can be utilized also. There are pop over ads, pop under ads, shape of a fly ad, etc. The fonts and colors of the ads can also be edited. There is built-in tracking for the sign-up form and also for the messages.

Getresponse

One of the major advantages of this software is that it provides a free marketing tutorial. Also, you are provided with excellent telephone technical support. Every aspect of the emails sent out are quanified and tracked, which helps in identifying the weaker areas of your marketing plan.

The tracking the provide ranges from email clicks, how many emails were opened, as well as correlation to sales in real time. There is the form builder, which enables you to build engaging web forms only with few clicks. There are as many as 500 templates which save time on template design. The email marketing can also be tracked using your iPhone. The platform also includes features like email-to-speech, video email marketing, online surveys, and much more which help boosting your business.

Infusionsoft

Infusionsoft not only helps with internet marketing, but also has a customer relationship management system (CRM) along with email marketing. In this system, all details about the leads are tracked. These details and feedback on effectiveness are of immense help in sending out targeted emails, which lead to increased sales. It includes a smart automation system that enables you to send out specific messages to a prospective customer, depending on the customers response and background. It is also equipped with an Open API (application programming interface), which allows system integration with other platforms, apps, and other online addons. This also facilitates easy import or export of contacts.

Plx Autoresponder v3.8

This autoresponder script can be used on Linux, Unix, and Windows platforms. The only potential drawback in using this software is that you should be well-versed with scripts. Also, images cannot be sent. Therefore, if your email marketing strategies include sending images, then this is not the right option for you.

Before you buy any one, it is important that you decide what your business needs and an autoresponder may fit into your plans now and for the future. Using a trial version to test them out makes sense if you are just not sure. It will help you assess the usability and necessity before you actually invest and commit time to integrating to one of them.

How to Choose the Best Email Marketing Software

Choose According To Your Needs

Many email marketing softwares, known as integrated softwares, can work in seemless integration with your current Customer Relationship Management (CRM) system. CRM's can be more expensive than the standalone marketing software. It is for you to decide whether you need a standalone or integrated system, depending on your business needs.

The need to reach out to customers, while you are running your business is at the utmost priority. In management studies, marketing is seen as the key to success. Marketing provides various options to get noticed and keep your business top of mind with your customers. It is only when a firm gets noticed, will it get business from its target customers. Emails, advertisements, SMS, digital banners, etc are some of the most common marketing strategies that are used to get noticed and stay at the forefront of your customer's mind.

Email marketing, as the name suggests, is the marketing strategy that uses the medium of email to reach out to customers. Your current customer base or the purchased lists you have acquired contain the email addresses of your customers and potential customers. In case you wish to do the marketing yourself, instead of hiring a third-party, you will need a reliable marketing software which can perform the task in minutes to help you win more business.

Eight Factors to Consider

Evaluate Your Business Needs

There are hundreds of email marketing softwares which are available. Each of these softwars has its own specialization. Few softwares can capture email addresses, manage the emails, send out emails, and also analyze responses after a stipulated time period. It is for you to decide whether you need a software to perform all these tasks for you, or which tasks you need individually for the needs of your business. Carefully research the features of the softwares, and then narrow down on any one of them and match them against your business needs.

Upgrades

Computer and internet technology are constantly changing. If the software that you have currently chosen doesn't adhere to this changing process, your software may soon become outdated. This can adversely effect your business. Thus, it is necessary to have a software that upgrades itself on a regular basis as the technology it interfaces with changes.

Ease of Use

The software that you choose will be used by many employees of your firm. If using the software needs expertise, the likelihood of being used to its fullest extent will be reduced. Thus, the ease of using the software plays a vital role in choosing the software that's right for your business. It should have a simple user interface with an easy troubleshooting or help option.

Features

Email marketing softwares are created to give end-to-end marketing solutions. From the import of contact lists to sending the email, all the tasks should be performed by the software. The software should be able to detect repeated addresses and filter them out. Also, many softwares allow you to tag address depending on the geographic area, so that demographic-specific emails can be sent. However, as I mentioned earlier, it is advisable to evaluate your feature-related needs before zeroing-in on any particular software.

Cost

Though all the other factors matter, it eventually boils down to the cost of the email marketing solution. When you have just started a business or when you are in the beginning stages of growing your business, the fund allocation for the marketing campaign is not huge. Thus, it is necessary to consider the cost-effectiveness of the software before buying it.

Help and Support

Once you have bought the software, there are bound to be glitches in its usage. Your problems need to be solved in a timely manner by the software development company. A representative from the firm should be available for help, through features like live chat. Consult with existing or past customers of these developers to find out about their after-sales support.

Integrating With Social Media

Social media is the newest hangout place, and often potential customers are found on this platform. Thus, it is wise to tap this sector for marketing purposes. There are many softwares available in the market which can integrate emails with social media like Facebook, Twitter, Google+, etc. This integration will definitely garner you more customers due to the social media website's user base.

Report Creation

The need to use an email marketing software to make customers aware of your product through an email. It is only when you know how effective the campaign is, that you can make amendments to it and plan out your future strategy. The software should provide you all the graphs and charts regarding the subscription to the email, unsubscribing information, how many people actually opened the email, how many emails reached the intended customer, etc.

You will find a lot of email marketing software reviews online, read each of them carefully by keeping the said factors in mind. By using such a software, you will be able to grow your business in the digital marketplace as well.

About the Author, Paul D. Kings

Paul D. Kings is a software engineer, father, husband, and self-published author. He likes to write about selling and making money online. Paul has been selling on eBay and Amazon since 2007.

Visit Paul's website at https://www.pauldkings.com

Want to Read More?
Find my other books at:
https://www.pauldkings.com

Free Training:

"How to Earn a 6-Figure Side-Income Online"

One Last Thing...

If you enjoyed this book or found it useful I'd be very grateful if you'd post a short review on Amazon. Your support really does make a difference and I read all the reviews personally so I can get your feedback and make this book even better.

Thanks again for your support!

www.ingramcontent.com/pod-product-compliance
Lightning Source LLC
Chambersburg PA
CBHW070859070326
40690CB00009B/1911